THE MYSTERY OF

THE MYSTERY OF CHRIST

Meditations and prayers

Keith Ward

First published in Great Britain in 2018

Society for Promoting Christian Knowledge
36 Causton Street
London SW1P 4ST
www.spck.org.uk

British Library Cataloguing-in-Publication Data
A catalogue record for this book is available from the British Library

ISBN 978–0–281–07915–5
eBook ISBN 978–0–281–07916–2

Typeset by Fakenham Prepress Solutions, Fakenham, Norfolk NR21 8NN
First printed in Great Britain by Ashford Colour Press
Subsequently digitally reprinted in Great Britain

eBook by Fakenham Prepress Solutions

Produced on paper from sustainable forests

Contents

Contents

Introduction

It may be held that little can be known with certainty about the historical Jesus, though it seems very probable that he was a charismatic peripatetic teacher and healer, who gathered a band of devoted disciples around him. He criticized the hypocrisy of religious leaders, he socialized with outcasts and the disreputable, and he interpreted Jewish law in a humane way, without abandoning it. It also seems likely that he was crucified because it was thought that he claimed to be King of the Jews, a messianic figure who preached the advent of the rule of God in Israel. It is virtually certain that some disciples had a strong sense that he had risen from death, that his Spirit transformed their lives, that he reigned with God, and that he would return as the judge of the world. Jesus came to be seen as a spiritual king through whom God's rule, the rule of the Spirit, had been inaugurated in a new way.

What the nature of Jesus' reign and of his return was remained unclear. But he quickly came to be taken as a true image of God, as one whose character placed human lives under judgement, and whose death and resurrection offered deliverance from moral and natural evil. So he was worshipped as the human image of the divine, who forgave sin and enabled divine love to transform the lives of his devotees and make them one with God. His disciples looked forward to a time when God's rule of love would be complete and evil would be finally eliminated.

Out of the memories of his life and teachings, an image was formed of a heavenly figure, 'Christ crucified and risen', who expresses the self-giving love of God, through whom the world is judged, and by whom life with God is offered to those who give their lives to serve him. Christians believe this to be an authentic image of God that has arisen from the historical person of Jesus. In the Bible it is expressed in the mytho-logical language of traditional Hebrew poetic thought about the origin and goal of all things. There are people to whom that language no longer speaks; it is for them too replete with ancient legends, anthropocentric views of the cosmos, and the supernatural fantasies of a mythic world view. People now have what sometimes seems to be a new mythology, evoked by the scientific picture of a vast and evolving cosmos. But the transformative image of divine love as the origin and goal of the cosmos, and the image of the self-giving, self-realizing and self-transforming Christ, can still retain its ancient power in this new cosmic context. This image of the divine reality is able to expose the moral failings of humanity, but also offers forgiveness and enables men and women to live with hope and to be more loving, creative, compassionate and joyful.

This book is a set of meditations on biblical images of Christ, placed in the context of the new cosmic world view. It is a series of reflections and prayers on the central mystery of the Christian faith, the mystery of Christ. By this I mean not that it is an unsolved puzzle but that it is the presentation of a truth that reveals the deepest meaning of human existence. That truth can never be fully grasped by human minds, for the reality of God, which is infinite, cannot be comprehended by using the limited concepts of human languages. But a sense of it can be evoked by acts and images. By reflection on the images of Christ in the Gospels, a sense of the mystery of Christ's eternal being can be evoked. The mystery of Christ, beyond but never contradicting reason, is the revelation of the unlimited love of God in and through the life of Jesus of Nazareth.

If Christian theology is the attempt to formulate some understanding of God, however inadequately, then this is a Christian theology. But it is a theology written as prayer, and the price of that is it works, if it does, by hints, implications and invitations to personal reflection, based on a particular reading of Scripture. It concentrates on the Gospels, as the only record of the life and teachings of Jesus that we have. I have treated the Gospels as vehicles for the presentation of a set of positive spiritual truths, based on memories of Jesus and experiences of the risen Christ within the early Christian movement. It is meant to serve as material for reflection and meditation. Jesus Christ was believed by his disciples to be the image and expression in human form of the infinite and invisible God, and the records of his life and teachings are attempts to bring out something of what is involved in that image. I have set out to provide one theologically informed set of reflections from my own time and place on what I believe to be the unique and life-transforming revelation of God in the person of Jesus Christ.

I have said that my reflections will be positive and will concentrate on the spiritual truths that I believe are expressed in the Gospels. There are differing interpretations of Jesus even among those who take him as their Lord and Saviour. When I say that my interpretation is positive, I mean that it stresses that Jesus' proclamation of the kingdom is wholly good news, not a message of condemnation for millions of unbelievers ('God did not send the Son into the world to condemn the world, but in order that the world might be saved through him': John 3.17). His message is one of God's limitless readiness to forgive, of God's will that all should be saved, and of God's changeless concern for the ultimate good of all creation. Of course there is judgement and condemnation of sin, and that is a serious matter. But I take Jesus' message to be that God wills that all should repent and turn to God in trust (1 Timothy 2.4), and will help them to do so if they so wish. 'Mercy triumphs over judgement' (James 2.13), and even death will not frustrate the working of the love of God (Romans 8.38–39).

When I say that the Gospels speak of spiritual truths, I mean that they often describe spiritual (non-physical) realities in physical terms. I hope that what I mean by 'spiritual truth' will become clearer as these reflections proceed. My view is not that the physical events (like, for instance, in a particularly spectacular case, the raising of Lazarus from the dead) do not matter. It is that their real and truly important meaning is (for instance, in the Lazarus case) about the new life that Christ offers, in raising humans from the 'death' of greed and hatred. I know from experience that Christians will differ about whether such miraculous events occurred in the literal and very spectacular way described in the Gospels. I believe that the spiritual truth is what is important, whatever precise physical events occurred, though I also believe that the physical can be a proper vehicle of spiritual truth. So I have taken the Gospel accounts as they stand without any attempt at critical study of their origins and provenance, because I am primarily concerned with their spiritual import. From time to time I have added short sections on more radical interpretations of the texts, which are fairly common among many good biblical scholars and theologians, to show that they can still share rather closely the spiritual insights of more traditional readings. I have put these sections in a different font, so that they can be easily identified. There is a place for a fully critical study of the Gospel records, and I know that a range of differing views of such questions is possible, but that is not my concern here. I believe the spiritual truths remain, that they are what the Gospel-writers were primarily concerned with, and they are what I wish to explore.

I will begin with the Prologue to the Gospel of John, because it begins with the creation itself, and places Jesus in relation to that beginning, with his relation to the eternal Word or Wisdom of God. I move on to consider the life and teaching of the historical Jesus as it is recorded in the first three Gospels. I reflect on the main images of Jesus in the Gospels, which illustrate how the disciples came to see him as their Lord. Then I consider how Christ is seen as judge and saviour of the world, and so is given cosmic significance. I conclude with meditations on images of Jesus in the Gospel of John, which ends, as it began, with a view of Christ as the origin and fulfilment of the whole creation.

THE ETERNAL CHRIST

The eternal Word

———·•◆•·———

'In the beginning was the Word' (John 1.1). The Greek for 'Word' is *Logos*, which can mean reason, intellect or wisdom. We could think of it as an intellect or mind which knows everything that could possibly be. It knows all possible states of affairs, and so it contains the patterns or archetypes of all worlds. Nothing is beyond its knowledge.

'The Word was with God' – that mind of limitless knowledge arises from the ultimate source of all beings, which is beyond intellect and beyond human understanding and imagination. 'And the Word was God' – this mind is not other than God. It is the one divine reality itself, as it expresses its being in the form of mind and thought. The Word is the mind of God, eternal and infinite. The Word is Christ, existing before any universe existed, and is one of the ways in which God exists.

'All things came into being through him' (John 1.3). The universe was shaped in accordance with the patterns that exist in the divine mind, that is, in Christ. In the beginning of this universe, 'the earth was a formless void and darkness covered the face of the deep, while a wind from God swept over the face of the waters' (Genesis 1.2). When this universe began to be, it was a great and formless deep, called in Hebrew *tohu va bohu*, without shape or form. Physicists, though only since 1927, see it as a minute point of virtually infinite mass and density, from which developed what we see as a four-dimensional space–time. The universe was created as other than God. But God relates to it in three ways: first, as its source and Origin, the eternal reality, limitless, beyond thought and imagination, that underlies and supports the fragile structures of space and time; second, as Word or universally embracing Thought that contains the patterns, the blueprints, of all things that may ever begin to be; third, as Spirit, like a mighty wind, a shaping dynamic energy that breathes fire into those patterns and gives them finite material existence. God is the primal Origin, the eternal Word that is the pattern of all things, and the Spirit of wind and fire that shapes the primal void in accordance with that pattern.

In creation, the values that exist eternally and changelessly in God are given a new, finite, temporal and physical form. Within that creation, intelligent personal beings emerge which can share in their own limited way the contemplation and love of all that is true, beautiful and good. As parts of creation, they can appreciate and help to shape those forms in new ways, sharing to some extent in the creative activity of God, and developing societies of embodied minds where loving personal relationships with other beings could be realized.

The Bible says that when the universe began, 'God said, "Let there be light"; and there was light' (Genesis 1.3). Putting this within the modern scientific understanding of the origin of the universe we could say that the Word of God, existing eternally beyond the finite forms of space and time, conceived the idea of light. The Spirit of God shaped within the cosmic abyss the physical expression of this idea. Thus the universe was formed in thought and shaped in the realm of time, a realm poised between the self-existing reality of God and the half-reality of the dark and unformed void. The history of the universe began.

∼

Lord God, you are the creator of all things; enable us to be creative in our own lives and in our own way, bringing about things that are worthwhile in themselves and for all who can share them. Lord, help us to be creators of goodness.

Lord Jesus Christ, eternal Word, you are the pattern of all things and the expression of divine wisdom; help us to be wise in our dealing with the complexities of our daily lives, and fill us with curiosity to seek out and understand the mysteries of your creation. Lord, grant us wisdom.

Spirit of God, you are the power of life and love; inspire us to delight in the particular beauties of this world, to grow in the fruits of joy, patience, kindness and concern as we meet with others and learn to respect and honour their unique person-alities and their place in the divine purpose for the world. Lord, help us to love.

The image of God

From its dimensionless beginning, the cosmos expanded into space and time throughout millions of years and vast regions of space. The first atoms brought form and order to being. They generated complex and stable elements, and in the fiery explosions of stars the heavier elements like carbon, the basis of life, were forged. As planets formed around the stars, within the host of galaxies those elements seeded some planets, and growing and reproducing organic life forms came into being, the life of plants and trees. On this planet earth the process of increasing integration and complexity continued, and the many varieties of animal life developed forms of consciousness and agency. Finally, as carbon-based life forms generated ever more complex nervous systems and brains, one animal form gained the capacity to think and imagine abstractly and to act freely and responsibly. 'God said, "Let us make humankind in our image, according to our likeness"' (Genesis 1.26). From and as part of the life of the cosmos, and by the will and purpose of God, humans began to be.

We humans are made in the image of God not because we are physically like God, who is beyond all physical form, but because we can think with wisdom and intelligence, because we can distinguish between good and evil, and because we can act for the sake of goodness. God is wise, God is good and God creates the cosmos for a purpose. Though wisdom, goodness and will exist in a unique and perfect way in God, humans, however partially and imperfectly, share in these qualities. We can, in some way and to some extent, 'become participants in the divine nature' (2 Peter 1.4), and that is the destiny that God wills for us.

This human destiny, which is part of the innermost purpose of the creation, was made clear in the life of Jesus the Christ. In him 'the Word became flesh' (John 1.14) – the eternal took form in time. That which has no beginning and no end was born and died. That which is beyond all worlds and names was found within a particular place and with a particular name. The place was Galilee, a small rebellious outpost of the ancient Roman Empire, and the name was *Yehoshua* (Joshua) – or, as we know it in its Greek form, Jesus. The eternal archetype or pattern of humanity remained unchanged, part (if it is possible to speak of parts in the undivided unity of the divine) of the unlimited divine wisdom and understanding. But that timeless archetype, by the creative power of the Spirit, was made real in space and time. This was no contraction of the eternal reality into temporal form. It was the addition of a finite temporal reality to an eternal divine reality. The Word took a human body and mind and personality. That human mind and body was from the first intended to be a temporal expression of the eternal Word, the eternal in time.

From this we may learn three things. First, that the nature of God is wisdom and understanding. God is beyond our understanding, not because God is without reason or intelligibility, but because God's wisdom infinitely exceeds our small minds and conceptual resources. Therefore to seek God is not to believe in a non-rational and arbitrary supreme being. It is to seek wisdom and true rationality and clarity of thought. To know God is to have access to supreme understanding, and to begin to see the true reasons and causes of all that exists. Second, divine wisdom is not wholly beyond our grasp, since it has come to expression in a particular human life. In that life we see 'the image of the invisible God' (Colossians 1.15), a finite expression of unlimited wisdom. Third, that image becomes our guide to what human life ought to be and can be, when a human life is filled with the Spirit of God. More, the image of

Jesus becomes to us the vehicle of the Spirit's power to conform us, each in our own uniquely personal way, to the pattern of humanity perfected in Christ.

The Word came to expression in one particular human person in order that all human persons might (by 'adoption') become expressions of the eternal Word by following the way Jesus revealed and established. So the purpose of our lives is to be conformed to the image of Christ, or better, to let the Spirit of God conform us to that image. Yet we are given the power to shape that image in our own unique ways, and to be fellow workers with the Spirit in attaining a goal that is unique to each of us.

~

Almighty God, we are filled with awe as we see the immensities of space and time, the night sky filled with stars and the daytime lit by the flaming of the sun. You are the power that holds the universe in being and the love that draws the whole universe to yourself. Expand our vision, so that we may revere this world and this cosmos because it is the artistry of your hand, and expand our understanding, so that we may trace and love the wisdom that shapes the cosmos to be our home.

Lord God, you have made us to be the keepers of the earth that you have made. Teach us to have dominion over the earth as you have dominion over all things, a dominion of love, shaping the earth to express beauty, subduing the things that destroy, tending and caring for the things that fulfil life and health.

Lord Jesus Christ, we worship you as the human form of the eternal divine Word. May we shape our humanity on the pattern of your life, and learn from you what it is to be fully human, to live in God and to let God live in us. May we think with the wisdom that cherishes the beauty of the world; may we feel with the love that moves the sun and all the stars; may we act not just to condemn what is bad, but always actively to seek what is good. Thus may we grow into the image that you will for us.

The Word made flesh

Jesus was truly human. Indeed, he was fully human, because full humanity is humanity fulfilled in conscious knowledge of and loving relation to God. To have such knowledge of God is not omniscience, for no human mind can contain the limitless understanding of a being beyond space and time. But it is a clear and continuing awareness of the presence of God, and insight into the interior lives of other human persons. It is to have one's human insights deepened and extended, to have overcome pride, greed and hatred, and to have achieved union with an eternal mind of supreme compassion. It is to become a co-operator with that divine mind, in carrying forward its purpose for the world. To act in that way is not to be omnipotent, for a truly human will is limited to the capacities of a human body. But those capacities are transformed by the co-operation of divine power, which raises them to the highest degree. They become channels of a love that knows no boundaries or imperfections, and of a wisdom that is not impaired by self-regard and prejudice. Jesus incarnates the union of supreme wisdom and love within the limited forms of a truly human life, a life transfigured by eternity.

The human person of Jesus had a truly human form of experience, drawn from the senses, and it possessed its own creative freedom to respond to that experience. Yet the mystery of Christ is that this human person, full and complete, was so united to the eternal Word that it was untouched by sin – *hamartia*, the falling short of the perfection that God requires – and it was illuminated by divine wisdom, so that it could discern the purposes of God in the particularities of each historical situation. Such moral perfection and divinely inspired understanding is theoretically possible for human persons, though our estrangement from God has made it impossible in fact.

The first eleven chapters of the book of Genesis relate four ancient stories which embody the realization that human lives are not filled, as they should be, with the wisdom and love of God, and with a clear sense of the presence of a divine will and purpose. Adam and Eve, representing the first humans, try to take the 'fruit' of knowledge without first cultivating the will to goodness. Thus they turn away from relationship with God, the only source of true life, and they find knowledge without finding wisdom. The story of Cain and Abel shows how jealousy and hatred lead to murder. The story of Noah's Ark tells of how self-centredness and greed leads to death. And the story of the Tower of Babel points to pride as a major cause of misunderstanding and conflict between people.

These ancient tales are placed in the Bible because they make the point that at its first beginnings the human race turned away from goodness, love, compassion and humility, to ways of life that led to increasing estrangement from God and to spiritual death. That estrangement led to a general loss in the human world of a sense of the divine presence, and to the impossibility of achieving moral perfection, which some have called 'original sin'. That this was possible is the price of human freedom either to embrace wisdom and compassion or to turn away to the path of ignorance and indifference, hatred and despair. That this became actual is the tragedy of the human situation. But God will not permit tragedy to triumph.

Into this world, a world fallen from God, the Word of God united to himself a human person, Jesus of Nazareth, to heal the wounded world and reconcile it to the divine by the power of perfected wisdom and love. Jesus, 'born not of blood or of the will of the flesh or of the will of man, but of God' (John 1.13), was from the first a perfected human body and soul. His whole being was united, in a way that could not be impaired or broken, with the Word that was expressed in and through him, that shared all his experience and guided all his words and acts. God's purpose was that all human persons could be reunited with God and share in the unity of human and divine that was so fully expressed in Jesus. The divine Word shared our humanity so that humanity might by the knowledge of Christ's presence and the strength of Christ's wisdom and love share in the divine life.

~

Lord God, Creator of all things, your will is that we should form societies of wisdom and love, rejoicing in your world and creating new forms of beauty and goodness. We confess that we have loved ourselves too much and have not loved others as ourselves. We have sought knowledge without seeking compassion, we have been unduly proud of our own achievements, and we have been jealous of the achievements of others. So we have lost the sense of your presence with us. Forgive us and bring us back from this far country which we have unwisely made our home.

Lord Jesus Christ, in you humanity was united to divinity, and in you the perfection of humanity was restored. As we seek to follow you, fill our lives with your wisdom and power, so that as you live in us, we may grow to live in you. Drive from us the demons of hatred, greed and pride, and place within us your love, compassion and humility. Make us truly human, fulfilled in loving relation to God, as we were created to be.

Lord, Holy Spirit, bring to fruition in us what we are unable to bring about in ourselves, an understanding that is true, a love that is unrestricted, and a desire for goodness that is untiring. So may we become, however imperfectly, refracted images of Christ in our world.

God is love

The union of humanity and divinity in Jesus is unique and complete. Jesus said, 'I am in the Father and the Father is in me' (John 14.11). The human mind of Jesus was enfolded by the eternal Word, and the human sense of being a separate ego was merged in the consciousness of being one with an eternal mind. The human self did not cease to be; it had its own sense-based experience and creative agency. But it was, and was aware of being, a small part of a consciousness which was the basis of the whole universe. In other words, Jesus possessed the direct vision of God, in a way that is not possible for most of us, who are partly estranged from God by sin and self-regard. And that consciousness broke through in his words and acts: 'The words that I say to you, I do not speak on my own; but the Father who dwells in me does his works' (John 14.10). So it is that those who hear and respond to Jesus experience, each in their own unique way, a life-transforming meeting with the mind of God.

As a human person, Jesus is loved and cherished by the eternal God. He is aware of being supported by the love of the God he calls 'Father'. We can think of God as Father in a twofold sense. God is Father to the eternal Word, being the one who eternally generates ('begets') the divine Wisdom. God is also in a slightly different sense Father to the person of Jesus, who is the human embodiment of that Wisdom. God as creator is beyond all finite forms. Yet as the Word takes finite form the eternal Father becomes the lover of that which is other than the divine (the created human person of Jesus), even though that person is uniquely united to the divine Word.

This means that God loves in a twofold sense. In one sense, God from all eternity and changelessly 'loves' the beauty and intelligibility of the divine mind. Ancient theologians and philosophers had a word for that love. *Philokalia* is love of the good and beautiful. Such love does not need another separate being to love. For God is the good and the beautiful. God is, in this sense, what God loves. We can think of God as the supremely beautiful, as the one who knows supreme beauty and as the one who loves that beauty. These are three forms of one eternal mind and will, three ways in which that mind and will exists, so intimately bound together that they form one being. That is what Christian theologians call the immanent Trinity, the God who from all eternity has a threefold form within a completely integrated unity of being.

Christians believe, however, that the divine mind, the Word, takes a human person as its finite expression. Then the divine love becomes something new and different. *Philokalia*, the love of the good and beautiful, becomes *agapē*, a self-giving care for finite beings that are other than God and that depend wholly on God for their existence. Jesus, as a human person, is in one real sense 'other' than the eternal God, for he has limited sense-based knowledge and agency quite unlike the unlimited knowledge and agency of the eternal God. Even though Jesus is united to the divine Word in the closest possible way, he remains a real human person. So when Jesus prays, he addresses God as Father, as the source of his being as a human person.

Then God becomes the Father who loves and who is loved by the incarnate Son. The divine love flows into the created world in the person of Jesus, and that love, defined and expressed in Jesus, flows into the inner lives of created persons by the activity of the Spirit. We may then rightly speak of the Trinity as a fellowship of love, a fellowship that is not confined to the divine being, but also floods out into creation to embrace and unite all beings in cosmic communion. So it is that the definitive Christian perception of God is that 'God is love' (1 John 4.8).

Jesus called God 'Father' ('Abba' in Aramaic), but this should not be taken to imply that God is male rather than female. God has no gender, and therefore to call God 'mother' is also an appropriate metaphor. The term 'father' probably does originate in a patriarchal society, where fathers were the head of the family, and to avoid this implication some think it is better now to speak simply of 'creator'. But the term 'father' is enshrined in Christian tradition, and it seems more personal than 'creator', so I shall continue to use it, while stressing that it is a metaphor which does not imply that God is male or that males are superior to females.

Lord God, you are the Father of the universe and the Father of Jesus Christ. You give your being in love to the created world and you unite humanity to yourself in the person of Jesus. We thank you for the gift of life and for the loving relationship you offer to us through Jesus. We worship you as the creator of all things, the source of all being and goodness, and as the one who is the unlimited perfection of goodness and love.

Lord Jesus, you are united to the Father in perfect unity and in you we see what a perfected humanity will be. We see in you the image of the eternal Word of the Father, spoken to us in your life of forgiveness and reconciliation. We thank you for giving your life in obedience to the Father's will so that we could be reconciled to God, and we worship you as the one in whom humanity and divinity have been made one.

Holy Spirit, you take the good things of God and plant them in our hearts. You unite all creation in a communion of love. We thank you for encouraging within us the fruits of joy, of peace, of compassion and of kindness. We worship you as the one who inspires us, leads us to greater understanding of the true nature of our lives and brings us into unity with God.

Holy and blessed Triune God, we worship you as the one and only God who is the Father of all, the Word which unites humanity and divinity in Jesus Christ, and the Spirit who works to unite all persons within the unity of Christ. One God in three ways of being, knowing and acting, we worship you and give thanks to you for creating us with the purpose that we, in our small part of this beautiful universe, should know, feel and act as sharers and expressions of your being, our lives fulfilled in knowledge and love of you and of all things in so far as they are in you.

The mother of God

The Gospels of Matthew and Luke state that Jesus was born of the Virgin Mary, by the power of the Holy Spirit. This miraculous conception does not throw doubt on the full humanity of Jesus, whose physical nature derives wholly from Mary his mother. But it presents in a tangible way the truth that Jesus is also fully divine, the incarnate Word. As the Gospel of John puts it, he was born 'not of blood or of the will of the flesh or of the will of man, but of God' (John 1.13).

The dual nature of Christ, as at once human and divine, is hard to comprehend as an abstract theological doctrine, even though such a union is the deeply rational heart of Christian theism. So it is expressed by Matthew and Luke as a physical symbol, an event that is physically real but that has a primarily spiritual significance. Birth from a virgin is physically unique and extraordinary but not beyond the bounds of possibility in a world that is the physical expression of cosmic mind. It may be thought appropriate to signify the unique nature of Jesus as an unbreakable unity of finite and infinite, human and divine.

Because of this unity, Mary is described as the 'mother of God', not that she bore the creator of all things, but that she bore the one who was God in human form, the divine fulfilling the human nature, and the human mediating the divine nature, wisdom and power. As such, she stands in a specific relationship to Christ that no other human can hope to have. She holds a special place among the saints, those who live with the risen Christ, and she has become a sign of maternal love and mercy for all who follow Christ.

Mary was not divine, as Jesus was. She was fully human, and only human. Like us she was redeemed. The Roman

Catholic Church has made it a defined doctrine that she was immaculately conceived, though most other churches are not committed to that doctrine. It means that she was born without that tendency to sin and ignorance of God's presence that is the condition of most humans. As such, Mary was filled with the grace of the Spirit and without the imperfections of sin. She was what we hope to be, a fully obedient and loving servant of God. According to tradition, at her death she was 'assumed into heaven' – her physical body transformed into a spiritual body to live, and to have her own pre-eminent place, in the fellowship of those humans who have died and live in the love of God.

To call Mary the mother of God and to venerate her as a saint of heroic virtue and love is to affirm the unique being of Jesus as the person in whom humanity and divinity are united, who was born as human in order that we should come to share in divinity. The virginal conception of Jesus, as it is properly called, though not essential to our redemption or to the incarnation of the Word of God, is an appropriate symbol of the union of human and divine which is the central mystery of Christian faith.

There are many students of religion who think that the idea of a virginal conception is a later legend, adopted from stories of miraculous births in the Hebrew Bible and in other ancient religions. It is true that it is found only in Matthew and Luke and not mentioned elsewhere. It is also true that Jesus is spoken of as having brothers and sisters and that his mother did not always understand him. So the phrase 'the Virgin Mary' could be taken in a metaphorical sense, the sense in which Israel is spoken of as a 'virgin' ('Fallen, no more to rise, is the virgin Israel' Amos 5.2, rsv), that is, by analogy, a pure and innocent young girl, chosen by God and committed and consecrated to God.

Little would be lost of faith in Christ if this was the case, and in that sense the virginal conception of Jesus does not have the same importance as the resurrection of Jesus, which seems to most people central to Christian faith. Yet it remains right that Mary should be honoured and revered as the one who, in a unique way, knew Jesus from his birth, who witnessed his death and who experienced his resurrection. She remains a pattern of Christian discipleship, with a very special place among the human saints who stand in the presence of God.

~

Lord Jesus Christ, you were born not in a palace but in a stable. Help us never to despise or neglect those who live in poverty or want, but to remember that you were born not in luxury but your first cradle was an animal's feeding trough. Your birth was announced not to the great and the good but to shepherds in the fields. Your first gifts were not from the royal house of Israel but from priests of a foreign land and faith who recognized you as a king and gave you gold as a sign of kingship, incense as a sign of divinity, and myrrh as a sign for suffering. We worship you as true King of Israel, as the eternal Word of God, and as the one who suffered and died in order that we might come to eternal life.

Lord God, we thank you for the life of Mary, mother of our Lord, who hearing the words of the angel was the first to know the mystery of Christ, who bore Jesus in her womb, and so became the first of those in whom Christ lives. She watched over the child as he grew. She is the model of those who give their hearts to Christ. She saw at first hand Jesus' death and resurrection, and so knew and felt the passion and the triumph of the love of God. May Mary, with all the saints, pray for us now and at the hour of our death, so that we may rejoice with them in the knowledge and love of the God who became incarnate in Jesus Christ our Lord.

JESUS THE CHRIST

The Messiah

Mark's Gospel begins: 'The beginning of the good news of Jesus Christ, the Son of God.' Jesus, a young man from the Northern provinces of Israel, a country under the control of the Roman Empire and governed by a puppet king, was believed by his disciples to be the true King of Israel, successor of David and Solomon. As such, he was Messiah, 'the anointed king' – in Greek, the Christ. Many people hoped that the Messiah would end Roman rule and establish a just and peaceful Jewish state. But Jesus was not an earthly king, born in a palace, governor of an armed militia, supreme law-giver of a nation state. His kingdom was the kingdom of God, a community in which God, who is supreme goodness and love, ruled. The rule of God is the rule of love, and Jesus is the one through whom that rule is exercised. In him the kingdom is present and at hand ('the kingdom of God has come near', Mark 1.15). How does love rule? Not through force and compulsion, but through compassion and care for the poor and the oppressed. 'He has brought down the powerful from their thrones, and lifted up the lowly' (Luke 1.52).

So Jesus the Christ is the human being through whom God's love is fully and manifestly exercised, through whom a society is founded through which that love can be expressed. It is a society that does not rule the world by force and compulsion, but seeks to lead only by showing compassion especially for those who endure hardship in the world. Jesus is its King, as one who serves and is the pattern for a society of self-giving love in the midst of the militaristic and power-seeking kingdoms of the world.

⁓

Lord Jesus Christ, you are the pattern on which our lives should be formed. Help us to pattern our lives on you, so that we may, even though imperfectly, become expressions of divine love in our daily lives. Help us today to turn aside from seeking to dominate others, and turn instead to care for their good and for the fulfilment of the good possibilities in their lives. May we proclaim you as our king not by condemning and controlling others, but by healing, reconciling and making the places in which we live and work sacraments of your presence.

The Son of God

Jesus, the anointed King, is the 'Son of God'. In the Bible, this expression is not unique to Jesus. In Luke's Gospel, Adam is called 'son of God' (Luke 3.38). In the second psalm, said to have been written by King David, the king says, 'I will tell of the decree of the LORD: He said to me, "You are my son; today I have begotten you"' (Psalm 2.7). All human persons are meant to be sons and daughters of God. God watches over them and cares for them as a father or mother cares for their children, and the children are meant to respect and love their parents. But that loving relationship has been broken as human beings have chosen the way of self-regard and self-will.

In the psalm, God nevertheless calls the king 'son', overlooking the king's estrangement and imperfection, and adopting him into the divine love, accepting him with all his faults. Elsewhere the Bible records that King David was told by the prophet Nathan that God would raise up one of his descendants and establish his kingdom for ever. The same divine promise is made: 'I will be a father to him, and he shall be a son to me . . . I will not take my steadfast love from him' (2 Samuel 7.14–15). The special relationship established with David will be repeated for one of his descendants. Christians believe that this is Jesus, descended from David, and King of a new society of the love of God, the kingdom of God. So Mark's Gospel repeats these words when Jesus is baptized: 'A voice came from heaven, "You are my Son, the Beloved"' (Mark 1.11).

Jesus' kingdom lasts for ever, because it is not a national, worldly, kingdom at all, but a kingdom that endures for ever in God. Moreover, Jesus is 'Son of God' in a fuller way than David, because he was created without sin, free of the self-regard that estranges humanity from the divine.

There is no thought here that God physically generated a human son. Yet Jesus is not just a human person who is adopted by God as King and Son. For, as the writer of John's Gospel saw, Jesus the man is so fully united to God the eternal Word that he can truly be called one with God. The eternal Word is properly God's 'Son', in that it is a form of the divine and not the creation of a being other than God, or the creation of another (lesser) god. That is why it is said to be 'begotten', born of God and not just created as a different sort of being. The Son is a different form of consciousness and agency of one and the same God. It is the Word of God, and that Word expresses itself in the human person of Jesus.

Jesus the man is thus God's 'Son', as David was God's son, in that he is chosen and empowered to carry out a specific purpose – in Jesus' case, to express the divine nature and purpose in a human life. But Jesus is more than that. For the eternal Son expresses his being in the human person of Jesus. Jesus is thus 'Son of God' in one sense as the man chosen by God to inaugurate the kingdom of God on earth. In another sense, he is the human expression of a form of divine consciousness, not other than God but the very wisdom and compassion of God, which contains the pattern or archetype of everything in the cosmos.

Lord Jesus Christ, you were anointed by God to be Son of God, freed from the imperfections of sin and bound to the Father by unshakeable love. You carried out the will of the Father, even though such loyalty led to your death on the cross. We also are called to be sons and daughters of God, though we are not free from imperfection and our love is far from unshakeable. We ask you to send your Spirit into our hearts to draw us towards the perfection of our natures and to strengthen our weak attempts to love fully and truly. Help us to love God as you did and to know God as you did, so that we may grow into the fullness of the stature of your humanity. We worship you as the human image of the invisible God, divinity veiled in the mind, flesh and blood of humanity, and we pray that you will bring us to that unity with the divine which you fully possessed from the first moment of your human existence.

The Son of Man

According to the Gospels, Jesus referred to himself as 'the Son of Man'. The definite article 'the', present in Greek, implies that this is the description of one unique person. Jesus is fully and properly human. He is a 'second Adam', unique among men, born without sin, conscious of the presence of God and empowered by the Spirit of God. He has a human soul and spirit ('soul' can be interpreted as mind in relation to the sensory world, and 'spirit' is mind in relation to the spiritual world of values and of God). He is what God intended humans to be, and what, because of him, they might yet become.

In addition there is a reference to Daniel 7.13: 'I saw one like a human being [Aramaic, 'son of man'] coming with the clouds of heaven.' This occurred in a dream-vision, in which four great beasts rampaged through the earth, and were followed by one like a human being who, together with 'the holy ones of the Most High' (Daniel 7.18), was given 'dominion and glory and kingship . . . that shall never be destroyed' (Daniel 7.14). This 'son of man' is to be born to overcome the militaristic powers of the estranged world and establish an everlasting kingdom. There seems to be to the idea of 'the son of man' both a human and a divine aspect.

As 'Son of Man', Jesus claims authority to forgive sins, an authority that belongs only to God (Mark 2.10). He has authority over the rules for the Sabbath (Matthew 12.8), which were given by God. So Jesus has a more than human authority. He is a human person, but he is more; he is the human form of God. Though he is given an everlasting kingship, he is not a king who lives in a palace in a particular country. During his earthly life, Jesus moved from place to place, having no permanent home (Matthew 8.29). He ruled over no country, and said, 'My kingdom is not from this world' (John 18.36). His is a kingdom of the Spirit, and the powers he overcomes are those things that tempt human minds to turn from God to self. Those who hear and understand his words hold them fast in their hearts and bear within themselves the fruits of the Spirit – love, joy, peace, patience, kindness, generosity, faithfulness, gentleness and self-control (Matthew 13.37; Galatians 5.22). Such people form his kingdom, the kingdom of God, and it will never be destroyed.

Lord Jesus Christ, you are what humans were intended by God to be. Grant us a share in your Spirit, so that we might find it in our hearts to forgive those who oppose and offend us, to go beyond adherence to rules and discover the spirit of love and compassion that underlies them, to enjoy the good things of bodily life, to be free of undue attachment to particular places and possessions, and to be filled with the virtues that the presence and power of God can implant in us. Grant us the patience and courage to oppose the forces of hatred and revenge, and to seek the peace and fulfilment that you will for the societies of men and women on this earth.

The Lamb of God

In the Gospels, Jesus taught three times that the Son of Man 'must undergo great suffering . . . and be killed' (Mark 8.31), and he said that he 'came to serve, and to give his life a ransom for many' (Matthew 20.28). John's Gospel records that John the Baptist said of Jesus, 'Here is the Lamb of God, who takes away the sin of the world' (John 1.29).

The reference is to the ritual of the Passover lamb, a commemoration of the liberation of the Israelites from slavery in Egypt and of their eventual entry into the Promised Land. When the Israelites were enslaved in Egypt, on one night God ordered that each Israelite family were to slaughter a lamb, and the blood was to be smeared on the doorposts of Israelite houses. Then the angel of death would 'pass over' and not destroy them when a great plague raged in Egypt and killed the firstborn children of the Egyptians. After that, the Israelites would be allowed to leave Egypt, to freedom and the beginning of their journey to the land of promise (Exodus 12).

These things are material symbols of a deep spiritual reality. The world is enslaved to sin, to the dark forces of hatred, pride and greed. Those forces lead to destruction and spiritual death, even to the deaths of those who, though they are innocent, are grievously harmed by the evils of their society. We may feel revulsion at the thought of the deaths of innocent children. But if we see that as showing that sin brings destruction on innocent and guilty alike, we may find God not in the destruction but in the liberation of the enslaved.

That liberation comes through a self-sacrificial commitment to follow God's will and purpose. But the Exodus story expresses a sense that one cannot make such a commitment in one's own strength. Only a perfect life wholly offered to God can unite human and divine in love, completely removing all the dark forces of pride and hatred that make such a relationship impossible ('taking away sin'). So the life (the blood) of a 'perfect' lamb was offered in sacrifice as a sign of the self-offering that one desires to make but is unable to make on one's own. The blood of the sacrifice, smeared on the doorposts, symbolizes the desire to offer oneself wholly to God, a desire that cannot be realized by human strength alone.

Christians have taken this story as a foreshadowing of the human liberation from evil and union with God that is truly expressed in the perfect self-offering of Jesus, who was wholly united in love to God. Jesus gave his whole life as a sacrifice, an offering of complete obedience to God, in order that all humanity would find a way to such union. He makes the offering that we cannot make and he enables us to participate in that offering, to take it into our own lives as a growing liberation from pride and hatred, and a growing union of love with God. This is the beginning of true freedom and of true sharing in the life of God. To receive the perfected and freely offered life of Christ ('the blood of the Lamb') into our hearts is to participate in the life of Christ in glory.

The 'ransom' offered by the Son of Man is the cost he pays in sharing in the lives of proud and hate-filled men and women, and of facing up to their pride and hatred, which will inevitably bring suffering and death. It is a self-offering which opens up a new way of living for all those who will take into themselves the self-giving and self-transfiguring life of Christ, who truly participate in the risen life of Christ. We must do so, the Exodus account states, as those who are prepared and ready for a journey. That is to say, we must play our part as we receive the Spirit of new life and freedom, so that we may die to our old self and rise with Christ, 'with the new self, created according to the likeness of God' (Ephesians 4.22–24).

The Son of Man dies for us, that we may know true life. That is the measure of his love. 'No one has greater love than this, to lay down one's life for one's friends' (John 15.13). What we cannot do by our own strength, Christ does for and in us. The cost of that for Christ is the acceptance of suffering and death in the divine life itself. 'He has borne our infirmities and carried our diseases', so that 'by his bruises we are healed' (Isaiah 53.4–5). God shares in all our sorrows, and God's union with us gives us the assurance that 'love is strong as death' (Song of Solomon 8.6), and that death itself will not defeat love.

Lord Jesus Christ, you gave your life to suffering and death so that you could share in the estranged lives of men and women, and stand beside us in our sadnesses as well as our joys. We have nothing to give you in return except hearts filled with thankfulness and love. Help us to die to self-regard, pride, hatred and self-seeking, and to receive from you a new self of compassion and concern for others. Live in us, as the hope of a greater love that can be born in us because of your sacrifice and your triumph over the powers of death. Free us from the slavery of sin by the power of your life which has faced and overcome the terrors of destruction. You have shared in our dying so that we may share in your unending life. Help us not to betray your sacrifice by our petty hatred, pride or greed.

The resurrection and the life

'The Son of Man must undergo great suffering . . . and after three days rise again' (Mark 8.31). Self-sacrifice born of love is not in vain. As Jesus said, God 'is God not of the dead, but of the living' (Mark 12.27). What was unique about Jesus was not that he lived after death, for we all live after death. But according to the Gospels, he appeared to his disciples in fully physical form after his death. This was no ordinary physical body. It disappeared from the tomb (according to Matthew, before a large stone had been removed from the tomb entrance: Matthew 28.2). Though, if you take Luke literally, the body was able to digest a piece of fish (Luke 24.39–43), it was nevertheless able to appear and disappear instantaneously (Luke 24.31). It took a different and unrecognized form walking on the road to Emmaus (Mark 16.12). It appeared behind locked doors (John 20.19). And finally it 'was taken up into heaven and sat down at the right hand of God' (Mark 16.19).

The final phrase is crucial. God is not above the sky, God does not have physical hands and there is no physical body sitting next to the throne of God just above the clouds. The meaning of this symbolic language is that Jesus ceased to appear in this form of space–time and was consciously united with God in glory. Jesus was raised to a realm beyond decay, beyond the physical as we know it, where the presence of God is clear and unmistakeable, where the love of God is intense and overwhelming, and where there is no longer suffering or death. This is heaven, life lived to the full in the presence of God.

The miracle of the resurrection is, if the Gospels are to be believed, that this Jesus, Son of Man, appeared after his death for short periods of time in fully physical form to his disciples, to assure them of his continuing life and presence with them, to vindicate his role as God's chosen King and Saviour from sin, and to confirm his promise to them of eternal life with God.

The resurrection life is, as Paul said, not a continuation or resuscitation of a physical body (*sōma psychikon* – mind or 'soul' embedded in sensory experience) with its sense-based knowledge and its liability to the laws of physical decay. It is a spiritual body (*sōma pneumatikon* – mind or 'spirit', knowing and inhabiting a world of spiritual realities), directly knowing minds and beings of beauty, wisdom and goodness, an existence as different from the physical as full-grown wheat is from the seed from which it springs (1 Corinthians 15.35–50). This is the world into which Jesus has entered and which he promises to us.

> Some Christians think that the resurrection was not physical in nature, even in the extended sense of 'physical' (as a physical appearance of a spiritual body) that I have suggested. Yet they generally think that the disciples had a real experience of the living presence of Jesus continuing with them, even if this was not physical in nature. In other words, after the death of Jesus, there was a set of transformative spiritual experiences in which God was known and conceived by them in the form of Jesus – rather as God is experienced in the form of Jesus by many contemporary Christians. I think that such an interpretation would capture the heart of resurrection belief, for it would still affirm that Jesus lives in glory with God and that his life has become for us 'the image of the invisible God'.

∿

Lord Jesus Christ, you are the resurrection and the life. You are united with God in glory and your human nature is transfigured to be an everlasting expression of the eternal Word of God. We worship you as the human image of the divine and we acknowledge you as the Lord of all humanity. Help us to know your presence with us as the one who makes the infinite God accessible to us, and as the one who perfects human life by its union with the love of God. Lead us on the path towards such loving union with God, who is the origin and end of all things.

THE RISEN CHRIST

The descent to the world of the dead

'The gospel was proclaimed even to the dead, so that, though they had been judged in the flesh as everyone is judged, they might live in the spirit as God does' (1 Peter 4.6). The Apostles' Creed says that after his rising from death Christ 'descended into hell'. This was not, for Jewish thought, a place of endless punishment, but simply *Sheol*, the place of virtually all the dead. Many of the dead, however, are those who have been wicked and have not responded to God's love. One remarkable New Testament passage, 1 Peter 3.19, says that Christ preached to these 'spirits in prison', spirits who had disobeyed God in the days of Noah and so had reportedly been so wicked that 'every inclination of the thoughts of their hearts was only evil continually' (Genesis 6.5).

These were people so wicked that they had been judged worthy only of death and of 'imprisonment' in the world to come. Yet the love of God in Christ extends even to them. After their deaths, and in what was for them a place of punishment, Christ preaches to them so that they too might live in the spirit. As Paul writes:

> I am convinced that neither death, nor life, nor angels, nor rulers, nor things present, nor things to come, nor powers, nor height, nor depth, nor anything else in all creation, will be able to separate us from the love of God in Christ Jesus our Lord. (Romans 8.38–39)

Humans may reject God and turn to the greatest evil. But God will love them still, and beyond the grave Christ will proclaim the ever-open possibility of new life and hope for any and all who turn again to him.

Some Christians think that this is purely a piece of imaginative thinking, arising from early Christian thought about the destiny of those who die without knowing Jesus (after all, the story of Noah is almost certainly a legend). Even if that is so, there is a proper question about the destiny of those who die without knowing Jesus, and this passage seems to express a very positive belief in the possibility of their redemption.

Lord Jesus Christ, we give you thanks that your love is so broad that it reaches out to all people without exception; so deep that it speaks to call back to repentance those who have sunk to the depths of despair and evil; so high that it takes men and women to union with God; and so long that it extends to every time past, present and to come. We who rejoice in your love rejoice that love is not confined to us, but that we have the privilege of extending it to those whom we meet from day to day. We love because you first loved us; and because you have loved us we are able to love your creation and share with all we meet the love you have been pleased to share with us.

The judge and saviour of the world

'The Son of Man is to come with his angels in the glory of his Father, and then he will repay everyone for what has been done' (Matthew 16.27). Life in the world to come, a world where the Son of Man reigns in glory, cannot be described in literal terms. Physical imagery must be used, the imagery of thrones, feasts and clouds, of fire, prison and darkness. That imagery stands for realities that lie beyond the limits of the sense-bound imaginations of men and women.

There is judgement on the lives and actions of men and women. No thought will remain unrevealed and no action will remain unrecorded. We must take responsibility for what we have made of ourselves and of the world of which we are part. God, to whom alone all hearts and minds are open, will make known the innermost secrets of men and women, and people will be judged on the basis of their thoughts and deeds.

Jesus, who, according to the Gospels, consistently referred to himself as Son of Man, declares that this Son of Man is the one through whom the world will be judged. The imagery he uses, recorded by Matthew, is of a 'day of judgement', when the Son of Man comes with his angels, sits on the throne of his glory, gathers all nations before him and divides them into sheep, who enter eternal life, and goats, who go to 'eternal punishment' (Matthew 25.31–46). It is those who fed the hungry, welcomed strangers, clothed the naked, took care of the sick and visited those in prison who are regarded as sheep, and those who did none of these things who are goats.

The meaning is this: it is self-giving love for others that God requires. Those who have such love already share in the life of the Eternal, and they will continue to grow in that life in the world to come. Those who were filled with self-regard and ignored the needs of others have already hardened themselves against love. Their self-regard, which hates all others, will turn upon itself and become self-hatred. In the world to come, where such hatred rules unchecked, it will eventually destroy them utterly as the 'fire' of insatiable greed and self-loathing burns ever more destructively in their hearts.

There is a deeper, partly hidden, meaning in this picture. No human being, however wise, can be the judge of all the human beings who have ever lived. God alone can do it, through his eternal Wisdom, of which Jesus is the human image. The Son of Man is the one through whom divine judgement is declared. But this Son of Man is the one who gave his life as a ransom for many (Matthew 20.28), who came not to condemn the world but to save the world (John 3.17) and who is the self-sacrificial offering to take away the sin of the world (John 1.29).

Judgement is real, but it is not God's final word. The just judge is also the merciful saviour, and 'whoever believes in the Son has eternal life' (John 3.36). The justice of God does not delight in destruction. God always hopes and acts to turn men and women to repentance, to acceptance of the love of God which is always freely offered. For those hardened by evil, the way may be long and hard, but the way is open, even to those who seem to be lost in the fires of passion and self-will: 'If I make my bed in *Sheol*, you are there' (Psalm 139.8).

The picture of the last judgement reminds us that the demands of love are severe and inescapable. But God's justice does not demand death; it wills to turn our hearts to love. Therefore the divine judgement is delivered through one who took upon himself 'the punishment that made us whole, and by his bruises we are healed' (Isaiah 53.5).

Lord God, you are the creator of all things, and you have made us so that we could share in creating beauty and goodness in your world. You will judge our lives by the standard of self-giving love that was expressed in Jesus. By that standard we fail, and we confess that we continually miss the target of forming ourselves in care and compassion that you have set before us. Deliver us from greed, hatred and self-regard. Lead us to the life of joy and love that lies in our awareness of and realized desire for your presence. Lord Jesus Christ, judge of the world, regard us with your heart of compassion and turn our hearts to depend wholly upon you. Deliver all those who have in their lives rejected love, but who may yet come to see that hatred leads only to death and that liberation from death is possible only by accepting the love that you freely offer to all.

The ascent to heaven

'At the renewal of all things, when the Son of Man is seated on the throne of his glory, you who have followed me will also sit on twelve thrones, judging the twelve tribes of Israel' (Matthew 19.28). Having left this world, the human person of Jesus lives in unbreakable union with God ('on the throne of his glory') and is for ever the human expression of God. The world continues as though he had never been, ravaged by conflict, violence, egoism and war. Yet Jesus' disciples look for a time when war will end, when evil and suffering will be abolished and when the Spirit of life, of freedom, wholeness and joy, will found a new society in which love will rule. The kingdom of God will come.

This will be a reality beyond the imagination of sense-bound men and women, and it can only be spoken of in physical images that stand for realities of which we cannot adequately conceive. So Jesus paints a picture of a renewed creation in which the Son of Man sits on a throne as supreme ruler, while his inner circle of 12 disciples rule the tribes of Israel. Jesus is pictured as a king, but this is a king who serves and gives himself for others. The disciples too are to serve the 'tribes of Israel', the new Israel, all whom God has called into personal communion with the divine. Elsewhere in the Gospels the kingdom is described as a great feast (Luke 22.29–30), and again Jesus insists that the ruler of the feast is the one who serves ('If I, your Lord and Teacher, have washed your feet, you also ought to wash one another's feet. For I have set you an example, that you also should do as I have done to you', John 13.14–15). This is a new reality of those who know and love God and who are bound to one another in a joyful celebration of love.

In the renewal of all things, the whole creation will be transfigured, as the body of Jesus was transfigured when he 'ascended to heaven' or entered the spiritual realm, which is the unclouded presence of God. Such a regenerated universe will not be a physical replica of this one, shorn of a few minor details like suffering and decay. It will be the spiritual conservation and fulfilment of all that has been good, and the elimination or reformation of all that has been bad, in the history of this universe. It will be a new world, the apotheosis of the universe, its participation in the life of God. In that world, the Son of Man will rule a transfigured humanity and 'he will wipe every tear from their eyes . . . mourning and crying and pain will be no more' (Revelation 21.4).

Those who think that Jesus did not literally ascend through the clouds have in fact understood the deepest meaning of 'ascension'. For the presence of God is not in or above the sky. It is beyond this space–time altogether. Heaven is the presence of God, and those who exist in clear and full consciousness of God are 'in heaven'. Such an intense sense of God is rare in this earthly life, but most Christians believe that it is possible in the world to come, and in a realm which is not in this physical universe. Contemporary physicists often think that there could be universes beyond this space–time. It is to such a universe that Christ 'ascended'. It is one that we can scarcely imagine: it is not physical in the way that this universe is, though it is described as glorious and imperishable. The ascension is Christ's transfiguration into a more glorious form of being, not Christ's rising into the air. For some, such a literal ascent would be an appropriate symbol of ascension, but others may think it is probably a metaphor of union with God, whether in this life or in the life to come.

∼

Lord Jesus Christ, in you the kingdom of God has come with power and those who are perfected in love share your life in

God. We pray that your kingdom will come on earth, as it is in heaven, on an earth and a cosmos renewed and transfigured so that suffering and decay is ended and all things in heaven and on earth are sacraments of the divine presence.

Lord God, strengthen our hope for the fulfilment of your purpose for this cosmos, when nothing that is good will be lost and the sound of weeping will be heard no more, when you create 'new heavens and a new earth' (Isaiah 65.17), and we shall feast at your table with all who have learned love.

Lord, Holy Spirit, shape our lives so that we may become children of God and inheritors of the divine kingdom, and that we may bear in ourselves the first fruits of that life more abounding which we have seen in Christ and upon which we have fixed our hope.

The day of the Lord

'They will see the Son of Man coming on the clouds of heaven with power and great glory. And he will send out his angels with a loud trumpet call, and they will gather his elect from the four winds' (Matthew 24.30–31). The first sentence is quoted from Daniel 7.13 and connects the phrase 'Son of Man' directly with the heavenly figure in Daniel's dream-vision who ends the militaristic powers of the world and ushers in an age of justice and peace. According to the Gospels, Jesus claimed to fulfil the ancient Jewish prophecies of a coming Messiah and began his ministry by quoting Isaiah: 'The spirit of the Lord GOD is upon me, because the LORD has anointed me; he has sent me to bring good news to the oppressed' (Isaiah 61.1).

Yet Jesus radically reinterpreted these prophecies so that they did not refer to a political revolution, a literal freeing of inmates from prison, or to the triumph of the nation of Israel. His kingdom was 'not from the world' (John 18.36, RSV), and he said to the priests and Pharisees, 'The kingdom of God will be taken away from you and given to a people that produces the fruits of the kingdom' (Matthew 21.43). Jesus' kingdom is the rule of the Spirit in the hearts of men and women, and it is open to people of every race and nation. So the dream-vision portrays his angels gathering souls from the ends of the earth into his kingdom. But on the nation of Israel there will come a day of terror and desolation, as the Temple, the city of Jerusalem and the whole nation of Israel is destroyed. This is the 'end of the age' of Temple sacrifice, and the dawn of a new age when a people born of the Spirit 'shall be called ministers of our God', and 'everlasting joy shall be theirs' (Isaiah 61.6–7).

The 'elect', those whom God calls, are not called to an everlasting joy which is reserved for them alone. Like their Lord, they are called to serve the world in love, to be priests of the earth, treasuring it and all who live on it as the creations of a wise and compassionate God. Those whom God does not call, who live on in the darkness of a decaying world, are not lost as though they were without hope. Christ died for them, while they were yet sinners, and that death was not in vain. The love of God will follow them and, if and when they come to see what they have become and turn from darkness towards the light, God will go out to greet them and rejoice because they were lost and have been found (cf. Luke 15.11–32). That is why, though the 'day of the Lord' is a day when 'all the tribes of the earth will mourn' (Matthew 24.30), what Jesus brings is the good news that the love of God will ensure that goodness triumphs and that it is possible for all without exception to share in it.

Almighty God, we give you thanks that you have sent the Spirit into our hearts so that we may trust and love you as our Father and our Mother, and live as children of God. We thank you that you have called us to be priests of the Lord, interceding for the poor of the earth and bringing your gifts of reconciliation and kindness to others. We pray for those whose lives are blighted by the desire for power, fame or wealth, and for those who suffer because of such desires. Deliver us from the evil of attachment to the transient attractions of the world, and keep us in the companionship of those who wish to love goodness for its own sake and who find pleasure in your presence. For 'in your presence there is fullness of joy; in your right hand are pleasures for evermore' (Psalm 16.11).

The kingdom of God

'Truly I tell you, there are some standing here who will not taste death before they see the Son of Man coming in his kingdom' (Matthew 16.28). Many disciples misunderstood Jesus' teaching about the kingdom. The apostles James and John thought they could reserve a leading place for themselves in the kingdom (Mark 10.37), and Jesus had to correct them. Some disciples 'supposed that the kingdom of God was to appear immediately' (Luke 19.11), and Jesus in response told a parable about a nobleman who went away to receive royal power and left his servants to use the assets he gave them until he returned. When Jesus spoke of his death and resurrection, 'they did not grasp what was said' (Luke 18.34). Even after the resurrection, two disciples said, 'We had hoped that he was the one to redeem Israel' (Luke 24.21).

The problem was that some took Jesus' teaching literally, as concerned with freeing Israel from Roman rule and establishing a new national king. They needed to be taught that the kingdom was a spiritual kingdom, and that they had much to do before the King returned. Generations of Christians have looked for the return of the King, but they have often understood this as Jesus coming back to this earth quite soon and putting them in charge of affairs. Yet just as the rule of the King involved death and transfigured life, so the return of the King would involve the death of this world order and its complete renewal in a spiritual form. The world (the universe) will end and there will be a new world, but not before God has completed his purpose for this universe.

In New Testament times, people thought that the created universe was very small. Earth was its centre and the stars were lamps hung on the dome of the sky. The creation had existed for only a few thousand years and life had not changed much, nor would it change much in future. Ancient messianic prophecies had been fulfilled; the resurrection had begun; the Spirit had been poured out. Surely the end of all things must be imminent. However, in 1922 – as recently as that – Edwin Hubble showed that each star is a sun: there are 400 billion of them in the Milky Way galaxy, of which our solar system is part, and there are many other galaxies in the universe (an estimated 170 billion in the observable universe). We live on a minute speck in a universe that has existed for over 14 billion years and will exist for billions of years to come. This new knowledge suggests that God's purpose for creation is much larger than any biblical author could have guessed. Furthermore, the universe has changed enormously since it began, before there were any stars or planets, with the 'Big Bang' (postulated by an astronomer and Catholic priest, Georges Lemaître), and it may yet develop in unforeseen ways.

This enormous change of perspective changes the range and timescale of Christian hope. But it does not change the essential nature of that hope, expressed as it is in the many diverse images and thought forms of first-century Judaism. We cannot believe that we literally live in 'the last days', just before the universe will end. But we can believe that God's kingdom, the rule of the Spirit in human lives, came in the person of Jesus. We can believe that his kingdom came in a new way with Jesus' resurrection, ascension and the outpouring of the Spirit with power, and that many of his disciples lived to see it. We can believe that the kingdom exists in the heavenly realm, where those who love God live in the presence of God. And we can believe that God's purpose will be fully achieved, that evil will finally end and that the Son of Man will return in glory, in a transfigured creation, after the death of this physical universe.

Disciples of Christ are to be 'like those who are waiting for their master to return' (Luke 12.36). That means we are to serve him by acts of self-giving love, and we are to long for his presence with all our hearts and minds. We are to act as if our Lord would come at any moment, the spiritual world breaking through into the physical, the ways of pride and power being destroyed, and devotion to Christ being rewarded, only but completely, by the gift of his presence. And we are to hope that all creation will finally be transfigured and united in Christ, a transfiguration in which each person and everything in all creation shall share (see Ephesians 1.9–10). If we live like this, then we shall indeed see the Son of Man come in his kingdom.

~

Almighty God, you created this universe in order that new forms of understanding, beauty and goodness would be manifested in and through created souls. All the good things that come to be in the universe will not be lost and forgotten, but will be known and loved by you for ever. The universe will end, when all that you will to be done has been done, and the physical world will be no more. But the universe as it is transfigured in you is imperishable and incorruptible, and from it you will create a new heaven and a new earth, where the souls that have been born on earth will enter a new and greater life, where there will be no sorrow and no suffering, but all things will be irradiated by your presence and will shine with your glory.

Lead us to this unending life, where there is one all-suffusing light and one all-embracing love, where there is no need of sun or moon, for you will be our light; no sorrow or regret, for you will heal the pains of our past; no sense of transience, for all that is good remains; no anxiety for tomorrow, for you will deliver us from all evil. Lord Jesus Christ, we look for your coming in

51

the glory of your kingdom, and we long to see your face in the world that is yet to be. Help us to see this transitory world as the preparation for the imperishable world to come, and help us to see what we know of you now as no more than a dim foreshadowing of that time when we shall see you face to face.

THE COSMIC CHRIST

The Lord of the universe

'All things came into being through him' (John 1.3). The Son of Man will for ever be present in God as the human face of the eternal Word, even if that humanity is transfigured in ways we can hardly now imagine. But is that the only finite form of the Word? In a universe of billions of galaxies, and perhaps of billions of life forms different from the human, it seems that there could be many finite forms of God, each appropriate to some form of free and intelligent life in different planetary systems through the universe.

In the mind of God exist all the archetypes of being that could possibly exist. Among them will be the archetype of humanity. It is in this way that we can interpret Jesus' declaration that no one has ascended to heaven, except 'the one who descended from heaven, the Son of Man' (John 3.13). The Son of Man, the archetype of humanity perfected in God, existed as a thought in the mind of God, part of the living Word which was with God and which was God. When that archetype was fully realized in Jesus it could be said to be 'descended from heaven'. Intimate knowledge of the Word was present in Jesus in a unique way, so that he embodied heaven, the conscious presence of God, in his own human person.

What other finite expressions of the Word in our universe there may be, if any, we do not know. Yet we can see that the Word which is truly expressed in Jesus is vastly greater than anything we can conceive. In worshipping Jesus we also worship that archetype of all perfected creation which is in the Word. And we can begin to see what the letter to the Ephesians means by saying that 'he has made known to us the mystery of his will . . . as a plan for the fullness of time, to gather up all things in him, things in heaven and things on earth' (Ephesians 1.9–10). The Word is not only the archetype of being. It is also the fulfilment of being, by whom all things hold together, towards whom they are all directed and in whom they are all united. When the primal archetypes contained in the Word have been realized in the created universe, they will be brought to share in the divine nature, now completed and fulfilled. As the eternal Word was made flesh in the person of Jesus and raised to glory, so the universe itself will realize the manifold thoughts of God in the world of space and time, and be raised to share in the divine Word, which conceives, reconciles and completes not just the human race but all created things, all things in heaven and on earth.

The Christ, which we understand at first to be the anointed king of the Jews, is seen in the synoptic Gospels to be the Lord and redeemer of the earth, and in John's Gospel and the New Testament letters Christ is recognized as the Lord of the whole universe, of 'things visible and invisible, whether thrones or dominions or rulers or powers' (Colossians 1.16). 'Through him God was pleased to reconcile to himself all things, whether on earth or in heaven, by making peace through the blood of his cross' (Colossians 1.20), that is, through his life which manifested the divine self-sacrificial love. On earth this culminated in the death of a man on a Roman cross. In the universe we do not know what forms the manifestation of God's reconciling love might take, but we know that it will be whatever is appropriate to unite an often estranged universe to its creative origin and its final goal.

∽

Lord Jesus Christ, you are the one through whom all things have been created. We see in you a true form of that creative love for the sake of which the universe was brought to be. Expand our vision, so that we can see you in all things. All things in heaven and earth, in billions of stars and galaxies, are formed in your image, and when the story of this cosmos is completed they are destined to be united and gathered up in you, not falling into emptiness but transfigured into glory.

Lord Jesus Christ, you are the one in whom all things will be completed. Your love patiently and unremittingly draws all things, however far they have fallen away from your purpose for them, back to their source. In the end, the universe will be taken into your life, there to become what it was from eternity predestined to be, an expression of your creative love in a communion of shared experience and action. Help us to see our daily lives as expressions of your creative will, to make each moment transparent to your presence, and to see the good things we do, however small, as made eternal in your unending life. Lord Jesus, live in us, so that we may live in you.

The light of the world

'In him was life, and the life was the light of all people' (John 1.4). The light came into the world in Jesus, but it exists eternally in the Word. Jesus was known in person to a small group of people in the Middle East, but the light is the light of all people, throughout the whole history of the earth. It is the light of every intelligent and free creature in all creation. Christians believe that every person who is ever born is touched by the light of Christ, that light which brings understanding of truth, appreciation of beauty, the insistent demand of justice and the attraction of goodness. To attain to truth, beauty and goodness is to live a fulfilled life. But the light shines in a darkened world, where such attainment is rare and difficult, and the way to it is often hard and dangerous. Those who love darkness – who do not care for truth, beauty or goodness – fear the light, and those who live in the night avoid the day.

'God did not send the Son into the world to condemn the world, but in order that the world might be saved through him . . . And this is the judgement, that the light has come into the world, and people loved darkness rather than light' (John 3.17, 19). The Father 'sends' the Son, not as another, but as the divine life itself, in its form as the Word – the archetype, the realization and the apotheosis of creation.

The world lies in darkness, for it is an open and emergent reality that was designed to develop through its own inherent powers and generate persons who through disciplined striving could realize new forms of value and goodness. In their freedom to create the future, humans have chosen the way of attachment to self-centred desire, a way that leads into the darkness of pride, hatred, greed and ignorance. Yet the light of Christ is never absent, and, while it is present in everyone, in Jesus it is bright and clear. It foreshadows a world which 'has no need of sun or moon to shine on it, for the glory of God is its light . . . and there will be no night' (Revelation 21.23, 25). All the world can be saved, brought into light, when the darkness has been burned away and when all things become transparent to the glory of God.

Many biblical scholars think that John's Gospel, which contains long speeches by Jesus openly proclaiming his uniquely divine nature, is so different from the first three Gospels, in which Jesus speaks in parables and tells the disciples not to say he is the Messiah (Mark 8.30), that John does not provide a description of what the historical Jesus actually said. Instead, John is exploring the mystery of the person of Jesus from within a particular group of Christian disciples after the resurrection and putting his reflections into the mouth of Jesus.

If this is so, the Johannine speeches can best be taken as profound meditations on the nature and role of Christ crucified and risen, which have deeply influenced Christian thought throughout the ages and which give inspired insights into the mystery of Christ. On this interpretation, when in John's Gospel we read, 'Jesus said, I am . . .', we must take that as meaning something like, 'In the light of the resurrection, we can see that Jesus is . . .'. The spiritual truth remains.

∾

You, O Christ, are the light of all who are born into the world. We are tormented by greed, desiring possessions and self-regarding pleasure, by pride, desiring status and privilege, by hatred, fearful of those who are different from us, and by ignorance, slow to learn and misled by over-simplified definitions and descriptions. Yet your light of wisdom and compassion is within us and can guide us towards a greater passion for what is of lasting value, greater humility, more genuine concern for others and thirst for deeper understanding of truth.

We are often lost in the illusions and appearances of the world. Lead us to the vision of the Real and the True, that whose goodness cannot be lost and whose reality is unchanging. Lord Jesus, help us to find in your life the manifestation of the love that moves the stars and the wisdom that orders the universe to goodness. Send your Spirit to us, so that we may see truly and act justly, and in some small measure reflect your light on the world in which we live. Recognizing your presence and your beauty in all we encounter, may we learn not to condemn the darkness, but rather to look for the breaking of day, when all things will rejoice in morning light.

The way, the truth and the life

Jesus said, 'I am the way, and the truth, and the life. No one comes to the Father except through me' (John 14.6). The Son is the manifestation of the eternal Word. That manifestation shows 'the truth' about the nature of ultimate reality. It is the un-veiling (*alētheia*) of the personal reality of wisdom and compassion that underlies the manifold appearances of the world – 'God is true' (John 3.33). Jesus' own person shows the truth about God, that God is a God of universal love.

Jesus also shows what true human life is – a life filled with the knowledge of the presence of God, with the love of the beauty and wisdom of God, and with the healing and reconciling power of the love of God. And he is the way to that deeper truth and that fuller life. For in following him, and letting the Spirit which filled his life enter into our own innermost selves, we draw closer to God, and the story of our lives becomes the story of an infinite journey into God.

If that journey is in fact a drawing nearer to a God of universal love, then we cannot think that God's love is limited to just a few people who happen to have heard of Jesus of Nazareth. It must be that God's love is extended without limit to all who are able to respond to it. So what is meant by saying, 'No one comes to the Father except through me'? The one who speaks these words is the one who, in John's Gospel, says, 'Before Abraham was, I am' (John 8.58), and who says, 'I am in the Father and the Father is in me' (John 14.10). He is a human being indeed, but one whose life expresses the truth, wisdom and love of God. It is the way of truth, wisdom and love that is the only way to the true God. There is no other way to God, and if any think they serve God by violence, intolerance and hatred, they are mistaken.

The way to God is not easy, because it is not easy to be truthful and honest in all one's dealings with others. It is not easy to try to understand those who differ from oneself in so many ways, and to consider their desires and aims with dispassionate and unselfish fairness. It is not easy to be concerned about others, even our enemies, and seek their good as well as our own. Yet, Jesus says, that is the only way to draw near to God. It is Jesus' life which shows us that way, and his teachings which call us to follow that way. In the end, it is only his Spirit and his risen presence that can guide us on that way.

Jesus is the authentic expression of the way of truth, wisdom and love. All persons, wherever they live and whatever forms they take, are called to follow that way. Even if they do not know that Christ is the way, he is the one who calls and guides them. As Jesus was not recognized by the disciples on the road to Emmaus (Luke 24.16), so Christ may come to many hidden and unrecognized. Yet as persons come near to God, perhaps beyond the veil of death, Christians believe that all shall see who it is that has accompanied them on their way. It is the Lord of glory, who was truly embodied in Jesus of Nazareth, the way, the truth and the life.

~

Lord Jesus Christ, you have shown us the way of truth, wisdom and love which leads to the Father. Help us to put aside the lies and dissimulations by which we conceal from others and even from ourselves what we know and what we are. Help us to pursue truth, even when it is costly to do so, and be ready to overcome the prejudices and fears that prevent us from accepting uncomfortable truths.

Lord, help us to see ourselves as parts of a wider society which sustains our life and well-being. Help us to work for the flourishing of that society, so that people are treated fairly, the weak are strengthened, the strong are merciful and none are ignored or ill-treated.

Lord, give us a share in your compassion for all living things, so that we may see care for our world and for all life as part of our responsibility as your creatures. As you gave your life for the good of those who hated you, may we learn to give up a little of our self-regard for the good of those who are in need of things that we possess in abundance.

You are the way, the truth and the life. Help us to follow that way of truth, wisdom and love, so that all may have life, and have it more abundantly.

The one from above

'Before Abraham was, I am' (John 8.58). John presents Jesus not as a human person who was born at a specific time but as one who transcends time, whose being is eternal. The mystery of Christ is that he is both. When God was revealed in the burning bush to Moses, he gave no name but said simply, 'I AM' (Exodus 3.14). God is a reality beyond the transience of history, and yet who is engaged in history as the dynamic source of all that becomes, of all that takes existence from and depends for its being wholly upon the divine. In Jesus this reality is focused and expressed at one point in time. Jesus is for us the true image of eternity, and if we see him truly we see the nature of ultimate reality itself, so often hidden in the desire-distorted world of ordinary human existence.

So Jesus can say, 'You are from below, I am from above . . . you will die in your sins unless you believe that I am he' (John 8.23–24). We live on the surface of being, seeing only the sufferings and distractions of a world poised between being and nothingness. Jesus reveals the depth of being, for he unveils the incorruptible heart and mind of that which is eternal and immeasurably great. If people remain blind to that depth, if they are deprived of the only true source of all being, they will at last lose their hold on life itself and will die in despair. But Jesus offers a way to the eternal reality that is truly embodied and expressed in his own person. That way is open to all who can embrace wisdom and love. The assurance that this is so is the person of Jesus, who makes known the mystery of the universal love of God.

The temporal remains finite; Jesus the man is born and begins to be. But the eternal is without beginning or end;

there was no time when Christ the Word was not. In Jesus the eternal is expressed in time. The changeless nature of Being is expressed in and through the changing processes of time which make possible creative freedom and loving relationships. Jesus Christ is the paradigmatic disclosure of this universal truth. It is through Christ that the eternal is expressed in temporal form, and it is through Christ that the things of time will be taken up into eternity. 'Whoever believes in the Son' – whoever commits to living in Christ and letting Christ be formed in them – 'has eternal life' (John 3.36) – they too will find their life fulfilled in God and they too will transcend the transience of time.

Lord God, you are the source of all being, and everything that exists flows from you and depends on you. You are far beyond the grasp of our sense-bound minds, but you disclose your presence in moments of transcendence, when for a time things unveil a truth and presence that lies beyond them but seems to speak through them. In these moments the finite things of time seem to become transparent to the infinite and eternal reality that holds them in being. In such moments, human minds can be inspired to new heights of wisdom and insight, and can be capable of extraordinary compassion and love.

Lord Jesus, your understanding of the divine wisdom and purpose, your devotion to the felt presence of the Father, your acts of healing and compassion, and your sense of calling to proclaim the rule of God in the lives of men and women, were such that from the first you knew and felt that you were 'born from above'. Beyond the attainment of prophets and saints, your entire life, thoughts, feelings and actions were never contrary to the will of the Father, but always perfectly expressed the Father's will. You said, 'The words that I say to you I do not speak on my own; but the Father who dwells in me does his works. Believe me that I am in the Father and the Father is in me' (John 14.10–11). Because of this, we worship you, as one born of and filled with the Spirit, expressing in and through a human life the reality of God.

Lord, fill us with your Holy Spirit, that we may die to self and that Christ may be formed in us. Allow us to live by your Spirit, to express in our earthly lives the wisdom and compassion of Christ, and when our life is done take us to share in your eternity, together with all who have been drawn by love to be in your presence for ever.

The good shepherd

'I am the good shepherd. The good shepherd lays down his life for the sheep' (John 10.11). The twenty-third psalm describes God as a shepherd, who leads his sheep to green pastures. He protects the flock from danger, leads them in the right path and takes them to the waters of life. Jesus takes this metaphor to himself and goes further, picturing himself as the 'gate' of the sheepfold, which leads to life and wholeness, and as one who is prepared to give his life to save his flock from evil.

Jesus' human life is a living parable of God's relation to the whole of creation and to the human world. Jesus heals bodily and mental ailments; he teaches that God is a God of compassion and loving-kindness; he expounds the inward and humane heart of the Jewish law (the Torah) and exposes the hypocrisy of those who care more for outward conformity than for inward compassion; he establishes a 'new covenant' of love between humans and God which breaks all ethnic and racial boundaries; he mixes with outcastes and prostitutes and freely forgives their sins; he imparts the Spirit of joy, patience, kindness and love to his followers; he teaches and shows in his life that God's rule is not an imposition of unquestionable authority, but an enabling of service and unselfish care for others.

The image of a good shepherd who guides and guards his flock, even sacrificing his life in order that they may find fuller life, is used as an image of such a life. Christ calls his flock 'by name', and they know his voice. Who are the flock? In the old covenant, they were and they remain still the people of Israel, but in the new covenant, they are all who hear the voice of Jesus, drawn from the far places of the earth. As the divine Father and Son are bound together, so are the sheep and the shepherd. And there are 'other sheep that do not belong to this fold' (John 10.16), but who will in the end be brought into that same union. For Christ, the first generation of disciples came to believe, is the shepherd of all the earth. Now we can see more clearly that Christ is the shepherd of being, that is, of the whole created cosmos. While, and indeed precisely because, we believe that he shows us what God truly is, and binds us in love to himself, we also believe that he will guide and guard all who, in whatever way and in whatever form, from whatever time and whatever place, hear his voice and are called by name. For what the life of Jesus shows to us is a God of healing, forgiveness, universal compassion and unlimited love. Such a God will not turn away any creature who desires to follow him.

Lord Jesus Christ, you are the healer of the hurts of the world and the living expression of the loving-kindness of God. Protect us from all that hurts and harms us, and make us whole in mind and body. Teach us to act with care and compassion for all sentient beings, and free us from conformity to rules and conventions which confine the human spirit. Free us from undue pride of race and nation, and enable us to see all men and women as worthy of equal regard, and all life as worthy of our care. May we see your face in the faces of those who are despised and disregarded, who possess nothing and struggle to survive. May we not be judgemental about the lives of others, but be ready to forgive all those who oppress or offend us. Fill us with the joy, the patience and the loving-kindness of your Spirit. Help us to serve others truly and sincerely, not seeking to make them act in the ways we wish.

Lord, you are the shepherd-king, not compelling us to obey your commands but seeking to guide and protect us and always concerned for our good. You show us the heart of reality as a heart of personal love, which excludes no one and desires to lead all beings to fullness of life and joy. Help us to hear your voice and to follow you in living for others, so that our lives may be shaped in your image and we may dwell in the house of the Lord our whole lives long.

LIVING IN CHRIST

The seven signs

In John's Gospel, Jesus gives seven signs of God's nature and purpose as it is expressed in and through his human life. These signs show how human lives can be renewed, transformed and fulfilled when they are brought into a living and vital relationship with Christ.

First, at a wedding feast Jesus turns water into wine (John 2.1–11). Water is necessary for life. Wine is intoxicating and celebrates life at its most hopeful and joyful moments. To turn water into wine is to turn the necessities of merely existing into a celebration of fulfilled life. In the Old Testament, especially in the Song of Solomon, and also in rabbinic thought, the marriage of God and humanity is a symbol of lives fulfilled in love and in hope for the future. At the wedding of divine and human, united in the person of Jesus, human life is brought to joyful fulfilment and filled with hope that this union will grow and flourish.

Second, Jesus heals by the power of his mere word (John 4.46–54). The words that Jesus speaks call his hearers to the kingdom, the rule of God. There human lives that are marred by disease and death are made whole by the source of all life and being. All that is needed from us is that we should go out to meet Christ and ask him for the life that transcends death. Indeed, he stands at the door and knocks (Revelation 3.20), and if we open that door he will enter and we will be made whole.

Third, Jesus healed a chronically ill man on a Sabbath day (John 5.2–13) and was criticized for 'working' on the Sabbath and for telling the man to carry his bed on the Sabbath – both forbidden on rigorous interpretations of Torah. Jesus' response was to say that despite the Sabbath being a day of rest, God, whom he called his 'Father', was still working, and so he worked on the Sabbath too. But this work was not toil for money. It was relieving the sufferings of others, purely out of compassion. Such activity was, he implied, permitted on the Sabbath, and it was the activity of God. Humane compassion triumphs over legalistic rigorism.

Fourth, Christ is the 'bread of life'. Jesus feeds five thousand people with a few loaves and fishes (John 6.1–14). His risen life is food that is always enough, and more than enough, for a world that longs for life. Ordinary bread can become scarce or become stale, but the life of Christ endures for ever and is always new. If we come to Christ for nourishment, we will be freely given more than we have ever hoped for.

Fifth, Jesus walked on water, striding the waves in a storm-swept sea (John 6.16–21). The Old Testament says that God brooded over the waters of the great deep at creation. God 'trampled the waves of the Sea' (Job 9.8) and 'by his power he stilled the sea' (Job 26.12). So Christ stills the storms that disturb human lives and brings to safety all who are fearful and distressed.

Sixth, Jesus gave sight to a man who had been born blind (John 9.1–12). This was a prophesied sign of the Messiah, to give sight to the blind, and it symbolized the new vision of the meaning and value of life which Christ can give.

Seventh, Jesus raised Lazarus from the dead (John 11.1–44). Christ has the ultimate power of life and death, and can raise those who are dead to the world of the spirit, giving them a new birth into a life suffused with the knowledge of the presence of God.

These seven signs – of loving relationship, of healing, of compassion, of joyful feasting, of peace-making, of new vision and of new life out of the desolation of death – these are the gifts of Christ to the world, and they outline the difference that living in Christ makes to human existence.

Some Christians think that, while Jesus may well have healed many physical and mental disorders (since this is a gift that many people apparently have), these accounts have been exaggerated in the Gospels (as the lives of saints are known to be exaggerated and to grow more amazing over the years). Thus it becomes very unlikely that any human, however close to God, could change water into wine, walk on water, conjure food out of nothing, or raise the dead. Such accounts may have turned spiritual parables into physical events, and the spiritual parables may remain profound even if the physical events did not occur. Further, the accounts may be partly due to attempts to make Jesus perform greater miracles than prophets like Elijah and Elisha. In other words, some think that they seem to diminish the full humanity of Jesus and turn him into a sort of Superman.

Those who have such a view might point out that Jesus apparently did not wish to use miracles to prove his messianic status (Matthew 12.39: 'An evil and adulterous generation asks for a sign, but no sign will be given to it except the sign of the prophet Jonah'), that the impact of his person and teaching does not depend on the occurrence of such miracles and that we now better understand the limits that the laws of nature place on what might occur. The traditional view is that Jesus' unique identity with God would naturally make him able, by his unique mediation of divine wisdom and power, to have mastery over physical nature. But an account that is more sceptical about such truly extraordinary miracles can still sustain a belief that his recorded life is an image of divine love, and that God continues to act through him, through the story of his life, through the understanding of God that his image evokes, and through the liberation from pride, hatred and greed that his Spirit can bring. And that, it may be said, is the living heart of Christian faith.

Lord God, you have revealed your nature and purpose to us in and through the life, death and resurrection of Jesus. He is the sign of the unchanging presence which underlies the changing processes of this world. He is the unveiling of the future which you have pre-ordained for this world. He is the one who places upon us the demand to bring healing and new life to this world, and who places within us the power to fulfil that demand.

Lord Jesus Christ, the good news you bring is that we can celebrate life as an unfolding of loving relationship in which you never abandon us. Journey with us, and increase in us our knowledge and loving union with you.

You bring wholeness to lives that are broken and disordered. Enable us to find fullness of life, where our personal gifts and capacities can be expressed fully and wisely, and where we can discover the meaning of true health and well-being.

In you we find the spirit of compassion, not limited by rigid rules but fired by genuine and generous care for those in need. Help us to love others truly and to treat them with a care that goes beyond what rules require.

You invite us to a feast that nourishes and satisfies our deepest longings. Feed us with the spiritual food that renews our lives from day to day and always gives more than we can desire or deserve.

You still the storms of unruly desire, of anger and distress. Deliver us from unfruitful regret for the past and anxious fear of the future, and help us to trust in your forgiveness and the promise of your presence.

You give sight to the blind and replace our ignorance with patient wisdom. Renew our vision and give us hope even in times of seeming darkness and despair.

You can raise those who have died to new life. At the hour of our death, embrace us with your love, forgive us for our failings, raise us to life in you and take us at the last to be with you for ever.

The bridegroom

'The wedding-guests cannot fast while the bridegroom is with them' (Mark 2.19). The Old Testament prophet Hosea compares redeemed Israel to the bride of God: 'I will take you for my wife for ever' (Hosea 2.19). The prophet Isaiah says, 'Your Maker is your husband' (Isaiah 54.5). And the Songs of Solomon have usually been taken to express the mutual love of God and Israel as like the love between bride and bridegroom.

The relation between God and human beings can quite naturally be seen as the relation of servant to master or subject to king. But this relationship can be deepened so that it becomes like the relation of child to Father; as Paul says, 'All who are led by the Spirit of God are children of God' (Romans 8.14). The Prophets speak of a deeper relationship still, the relation of husband and wife, when two are bound together by desire – not self-regarding desire, but a mutual longing for the presence of the other, which expresses both an extension and a completion of the self: 'I am my beloved's and his desire is for me' (Song of Solomon 7.10). I give myself completely to the other because he wants me for myself, and he gives himself completely to me because my desire is for him.

This relationship of divine and human is a passionate relationship. It is not just a relation of the moving to the Unmoved, as Plato depicts the human relationship to the unmoved Good. God passionately desires the human being, and both human and divine are fulfilled in relationship to one another. In the Gospels Jesus is seen as the bridegroom, and he presents God's love in and through this human person. Jesus weeps over the fate of Jerusalem, and rejoices at the wedding banquet with his guests. He grieves over the loss of those he has loved, and rejoices at their return (Luke 15). He is prepared to give his life for his beloved, for 'love is strong as death' (Song of Solomon 8.6), and when love triumphs there is joy in heaven. In these things, Jesus is expressing the divine love, and as we respond to the person of the risen Christ we are responding to God.

Christ desires us, each one individually, and desires that we should be his. When we respond it is right that we should desire him and be bound in love to him. Now we are separated, but we long for this relationship to be realized in joy. This adds a new dimension to our relationship to God. Not only do we see in Jesus the pattern of love, which we should imitate. We also see the passionate love of God to which we are called to respond, in a union of self-giving and self-fulfilling, which discloses that to be truly human is to be in living relationship to a being of personal and passionate love.

∼

'As a deer longs for flowing streams, so my soul longs for you, O God' (Psalm 42.1). O Lord our God, we thank you that you have made your love known to us in and through the person of Jesus. Lord Jesus, you will be for ever the image of the self-giving love of God, healing, demanding yet forgiving, just yet merciful, reconciling, caring and compassionate, joyful and passionate. Spirit of God, place your love within our hearts, for 'in your presence there is fullness of joy' (Psalm 16.11).

Now we see you dimly and fitfully, but we long to see you face to face, and know you as we are known. Increase in us the knowledge and love of your presence, so that we may more fully reflect your love in our lives. Embrace us with the power and passion of your love, so that we may desire you above all things and find our fulfilment in giving ourselves wholly to you. 'When I awake, I shall be satisfied, beholding your likeness' (Psalm 17.15).

The bread of life

'I am the bread of life . . . Whoever eats of this bread will live for ever' (John 6.48, 51). Beyond the relationship of servant to master, beyond the relationship of child to parent, beyond the relationship of mutual love between divine and human, even beyond the love of the Father and the Son, there is something else. Something so strange and new that many pious believers in God, when they first heard of it from Jesus, turned away. Referring to the manna, the strange substance which was believed to have been sent by God to sustain the Israelites in the wilderness after their escape from Egypt, Jesus said that he was the true 'bread from heaven', giving eternal life to his followers. He goes on to say, 'Unless you eat the flesh of the Son of Man and drink his blood, you have no life in you' (John 6.53).

Though John's Gospel gives no account of Jesus' institution of the Eucharist, this seems to be speaking of that rite, in which bread and wine are received as the body and blood of Christ. Jesus says, 'Those who eat my flesh and drink my blood abide in me, and I in them' (John 6.56). The life of Jesus is not only something to be revered and imitated, not even only a life given for the sake of the life of the world. It is also to be received and internalized by his disciples, to become part of their inward being. Christ is to live in them, and they as a group are to form the body of Christ in the world, a living continuation of his ministry of loving service.

Great religious teachers give wisdom to their followers and show them the way to liberation from self. But the power of the eternal Christ is in Jesus, and that power is passed on to those who follow Jesus. Christ is present within them ('the flesh' is the local presence of a personal being), empowering their actions ('the blood' is a life poured out for the sake of others). So Christ is not only a separate person of incomparable wisdom and beauty. Christ is the true innermost self which is placed within the hearts of disciples, which can become their own true self, the God within – 'it is no longer I who live, but it is Christ who lives in me' (Galatians 2.20). Christ is not only the beloved bridegroom. Christ is the one who lives in us, and in whom we live, and Jesus is the one who makes this union of human and divine present in each one who follows his call. This is eternal life, to unite our lives to the Eternal, to share in and to express in our own unique ways the life of God. To many pious believers this has seemed too presumptuous for humans. But Jesus teaches that it is the free gift of God, the way to liberation from spiritual death, and to refuse it is to refuse the highest possibility of life.

∼

Lord Jesus Christ, you are the bread of life. Your presence brings eternity into human hearts. Eternal Christ, as you expressed your being and nature in Jesus, so may you be the pattern of our innermost lives. As in Jesus you poured out your life for the reconciliation of the world to God, so may you empower us to be reconcilers to God of what we see and know of the world. Enable us to abide in you, so that we may be your hands and feet, your healing presence, among those around us, and become vehicles of your infinite kindness and compassion. Abide in us, so that your life may be the life by which we live, and our union with you may be the driving power of our actions and intentions.

Lord God, you invite us to a union so close that we can no longer distinguish ourselves from you, but feel ourselves to be dissolved in your infinity. And yet we remain your creatures, with our own unique histories and perspectives. Poised between the dissolution and the fulfilment of self, our wills become partial refractions of a will that is higher than our own, and our thoughts become partial reflections of a wisdom that is greater than our own. We cannot claim that will and wisdom as our own, and yet we are parts of it, however fractured and imperfect. Lord, guide us on the unending journey into your infinity that your Word has begun in us. Nourish us with that spiritual food which made Jesus wholly one with you, and which leads us to become, in so far as we are in him, 'participants in the divine nature' (2 Peter 1.4).

The vine

'I am the true vine . . . abide in my love' (John 15.1–11). The vine, cultivated by God, was an ancient symbol for Israel. God trains the people of Israel to be the sign of his presence in and purpose for the world, committed to justice and to the pursuit of truth, beauty and goodness. Now Jesus takes that title to himself, summing up in his own person God's destined role for Israel, and, without denying God's covenant with Israel, opens Israel's covenant to his disciples, drawn from every race and nation.

Those who abide in Christ bear fruit – the fruits of love, joy, peace, patience, kindness, generosity, faithfulness, gentleness and self-control (Galatians 5.22) – fruits that, like grapes, are meant to make the hearts of men and women glad. Jesus stresses that such fruits are generated by the Christ within, who places his joy within them, so that their joy will be complete. But he warns that those who do not truly live in him, and do not bear such fruits in their lives, will be cast aside, like dead branches which are thrown away and burned. He speaks here of those disciples who are unloving, joyless, quarrelsome, impatient, unkind, ungenerous, untrustworthy, harsh or selfish. They will lack the joy of Christ and will face the purifying fire that burns away all that holds them back from truly sharing the life of Christ.

Vines do not live for themselves, but for the sake of those who drink refreshing wine and rejoice. So the disciples of Christ are called to live so that the world, and especially the poor and oppressed of the world, may rejoice. We are to pour out the Spirit of life for the world. Our calling is demanding, but its fulfilment is a joy that no one can take away and that endures for ever. When Jesus leaves the world his followers inherit the calling he gave to his disciples, to baptize the world with the Spirit of Christ's love, to warn the world of inescapable judgement on injustice, yet to give to the world the unfailing hope of glory to come and the promise of unending joy.

Lord, implant in us the seeds of the Spirit which will bear fruit in our lives. Grant us love, so that we may care for others selflessly and with a concern only for their good. Grant us joy, so that we may appreciate and treasure the life that you have given us. Grant us peace, so that we may overcome anger and seek to react positively to the problems that we encounter. Grant us patience, so that we may bear our problems without anxiety and endure hardships courageously. Grant us kindness, so that we may deal graciously with those we encounter. Grant us generosity, so that we may freely share with others the good things that we enjoy. Grant us faithfulness, so that we may be loyal and trustworthy in our friendships and our dealings with others.

Grant us gentleness, so that we may always consider the feelings of others and refrain from compelling them to act in ways that we prefer. Grant us self-control, so that we may act prudently and live simply without possessiveness or unrestrained desire. Grant us the unfailing hope of glory, founded on our knowledge of your transfiguring life within us – 'God chose to make known . . . this mystery, which is Christ in you, the hope of glory' (Colossians 1.27).

The Trinity

'Go therefore and make disciples of all nations, baptizing them in the name of the Father and of the Son and of the Holy Spirit' (Matthew 28.19).

This is the Trinitarian God of Christian faith, whose purpose for the cosmos originates in the Father of all, is expressed in the Son, the pattern of all creation, embodied in human form in Jesus, and is completed by the Spirit, the power for good that was in Jesus and that shapes and unites the cosmos to its divine origin and goal.

On this planet, the threefold God is known as Father, Son and Spirit. The Son, eternal and uncreated, the pattern of all creation, is present and manifest in the human person of Jesus. That person, transfigured in glory, remains for ever the human form of the divine. But the eternal Son is also present and manifest in the sacramental forms of bread and wine, as the sacrificial life, death and resurrection of Jesus is made present and effectual in many times and places. He is present and manifest in the hearts of those who place their trust in him, and in the society of those who, as 'the body of Christ', continue his work of love in the world. And he is present and manifest in the completed union of the whole cosmos 'in Christ', at the end of historical time.

This is the mystery of Christ, who is the eternal expression of the uncreated origin of all things, whose human form is the temporal image of eternal love, who lives within us as a power of wisdom and love that transcends our own, and in whom we live as we are drawn towards that final communion of being in God which is the goal of creation.

~

Lord God, you are the origin of all creation and in the depth of your being lies the source of all that is. You are the supreme good, the fulfilment of every worthwhile desire, inexhaustible in beauty and excellence. Yet because you have taken humanity to yourself in Jesus, we thank you that we can call you 'Abba', Father, sharing your nature and relating to you in a fully personal and loving way.

Lord Jesus Christ, you are the pattern of all creation and of what humanity is meant to be. Make yourself known to us in the breaking of bread, in our inmost selves and in the faces of those we encounter from day to day. Live in us, as we seek to live in you, and enable us to see you in all things, and all things in you.

Lord, Holy Spirit, you are the creative force that moves the stars, that guides towards the truth and inspires minds and hearts in thought, feeling and action. You are the inner companion who journeys with us and shapes us in the image of Christ. Be present with us, uniting us to the divine life so that we may come to know and love God ever more fully.

Lord, Holy Trinity, creator, redeemer and sanctifier, the origin, pattern and power working in and through this universe, known to us as loving Father, crucified and risen Lord, and inspiring Spirit, we worship and adore you. You are supreme truth, beauty and goodness, and you draw us to yourself as we move from darkness towards the light. Help us to live in trustful dependence upon the Father, rejoicing in the loving presence of Jesus Christ, and united in companionship with your Spirit. May we grow in the Spirit, so that we may die to the egoistic self, and our true selves may be raised and hidden with Christ in God.

In these short reflections, I have tried to show how the mystery of Christ originates with memories of the life of the historical figure of Jesus but expands into a vision of God as the transcendent creator of the universe, the incarnate Lord, human expression of the mind of God, who opens the way to the union of all creation and its creator, and the Spirit within human hearts who leads humanity on that way. There are various ways to interpret this mystery, and each age must find its own way to attempt to explore it, without ever claiming to have perceived the full and final truth. This has been just my attempt to place the mystery of Christ in the context of the new and hugely expanded view of our universe that scientific investigation has revealed. I believe this gives faith in Christ a depth and magnificence that is truly awe-inspiring, that takes the scientific view of the universe seriously and discloses the spiritual reality that underlies and upholds it. Seen in this way, the mystery of Christ takes reason to its limit and fulfils reason in love.